The Shadov

MW01204345

Copyright ©
Jeannetta Fuller, editor

Printed in the United States of America

First Printing, 2017

To my favorite
nephew AJ

The Shadows of A Man

Rashaad Fuller

(Righteous Sin Cleanser)

And

Harry Fuller III

(The Stone Thrower)

INTRODUCTION

This book is a reflection of my feelings and the "Shadows of Man" everywhere. It reveals thoughts that the majority of us do not have the courage to say.

Most of the selections in the first chapter were written in the late sixties but the anger expressed then is still prevalent today with a large degree of people enduring the same experiences. A lot of our society has not grown or changed over the years which makes these poems significant to today's anxieties.

After expressions of anger, comes poems of love and reflections of hurt and pain that remains a part of life that all must experience at some point in time.

The selection, Quentin, I feel is the height of humor and entertainment in this book.

Then you have the continuation of a man, his son. He will always be a shadow of his father in how he taught him to be a man throughout life. His mannerisms, the way he speaks, facial expressions, demeanor, charisma, integrity, being respectful and how to carry himself are the various shadows casted through his poems of life. He is a reflection of the Shadows of "A" Man through his father.

Table of Contents

SHADOWS OF MAN

GUARDIAN……………………..……..……Page 1

GIVE ME SOME TRUTH IN A BROWN PAPER BAG (FOR KELLY)……………………………..…….Page 4

IS A BULLFROG WATERPROOF?...............................Page 9

AIN'T THOSE HANDS COLD?...Page 13

ARE WE OR AREN'T WE…………Page 19

THE PURPOSE OF MIND………………...……………..Page 24

THE SHADOWS OF MAN……………………………….Page 27

MAKING LOVE TO YOU

for JEANNETTA......................Page 33

WOMAN.......................................Page 35

OUR
VOWS...Page 36

MY BRIDE...................................Page 38

OUR THANKS TO YOU..................Page 41

MAKING LOVE TO
YOU..Page 42

DELIRIOUS JOY...........................Page 47

REFLECTIONS

IRENE..Page 50

PERSEVERE................................Page 53

UNTITLED...................................Page 56

WINGS OF
LIGHT...Page 58

ONE + ONE + ONE =
THREE.......................................Page 60

MIRROR......................................Page 62

FINALE

TAKE YOUR
PRAISE…………..………………Page 64

EULOGY FOR
QUENTIN……………………….Page 70

CONTINUATION OF A MAN

COME WALK WITH ME……..………Page 77

PRISON TO
POWER………………………..…….Page 80

FROM GRACE TO
ETERNITY……………..………..……Page 84

MY WIFE OF
FAITH…………..………………..……Page 86

MY WALKING
MIRACLE………………………...……Page 88

MY HUMBLE
CRY…………..…………………..……Page 92

KEEP ME AWAY FROM THE
WOLVES…………..…….…..……………Page 95

LORD TELL ME
WHY..Page 98

LORD
W.A.R.S.................................Page 101

MY GUIDING LIGHT (for momma –
Jeannetta)...............................Page 104

SHADOWS OF "A"
MAN......................................Page 107

SHADOWS

OF

MAN

GUARDIAN

it treads the corridors

    of mindhood; your guide

    in your relentless quest

        for relevancy

it was given the responsibility

    of protecting your conscience self

    from your subliminal self;

    you from you.

        -i speak of your Guardian-

it is endowed with strength super/natural-

    power that far exceeds

    the nuclear abortions

    of man.

it is immense by any measure-

spanning the whole of your being.

it bears a strong resemblance to melancholy;

your personal/mental boogie man.

-i speak of your Guardian-

it answers to no man;

it is not bound by

the girdle of concern

for your petty desires.

it fears not the destructive forces

created by your ambitions.

it fears nothing.

with exception to

Vega:

-the point around which your universe
revolves

the center of creation.

-i speak of the Guardian-

it makes your manhood

a possibility,

your mindhood

an
inevitability.

post script—

conscience – that part of you
that is underdeveloped.

subconscious – that part of you
that is unexplored.

super-conscious – that part of
you that is your Guardian.

GIVE ME SOME TRUTH IN A BROWN PAPER BAG

I got sweet oil, motor oil, snake oil too

why I even got drops that turn brown eyes
blue

here's some reefer, religion, and such as that

right here I got an anti-inflation hat

look, here's a geodisic dome to keep you
from harm

an inflatable doll to keep your young ass
warm

a pair of these shoes will let you walk on
water

I'll let you piss in my pocket if you've got a ¼

come a little closer so you can hear me
better

what's that? It's a genuine gorilla-skin
sweater

this potion here will make your kids stop
cryin'

this chicken eye will let you know if a
person's lyin'

here's a piece of web that Spiderman used

and this is the stuff that made Lady sing the
blues

step up here and get your alligator salve

now tell me brother' what will you have?

-Just give me some Truth

In a Brown Paper Bag-

as I was saying before this person bothered
me

this elixir right here will make your dog climb
a tree

I got a hamburger that ain't made out of meat

and some mineral water used to shrink big
feet

this mirror will let you look at the back of your
head

here's a magic clothespin to keep you from
wetting the bed

I got Black politicians from the heights of
shaker

I even got a nuclear-powered coffee maker

this here's a correspondence course in
Motherhood

I can show you how Slavery done you some
good

I'll sell you a spell that will eliminate greed

or build you a house from one sesame seed

for only fifty sense I'll sell you a shah

or take out a contract on your mama-in-law

I'll sell you a formula that will turn lead to
gold

I'm sellin' seashore estates in the North Pole

come on and get your alligator salve

and tell me again Brother' what will you
have?

-Just give me some Truth

In a Brown Paper Bag-

as I was saying: here's a box of pestilence
and disease

and a recipe for wild rice and turkey knees

here's some powdered eagle lips to cure
your aches

how about some chit'lin' flavored shake and
bake?

now if it's your miserable life you want to
save

I can sell you 81 ways to cheat the grave

I've got this pyramid that belonged to some
king

look, I can sell you damn near any ol' thing

I've got everything, and you know I'm no liar

from vagina in a pouch to a Chinese lawyer

so if your money ain't got a whole lot to do

then brother, I really want to speak to you

now just look around and tell me what you
like

cause I'm sure we can make a deal that's right

hurry up and get your alligator salve

and tell me again Brother, what will you have?

-Just give me some Truth

In a Brown Paper Bag-

IS A BULLFROG WATERPROOF?

You speak of defiance (in mumbles &
whispers)
And you don't know what it means.

                                        or: maybe
you do.

That's why you're afraid to say it out loud.

Choking on that toxic waste that you've been
eating

    the first/last 400 years.

The perfect misrepresentation of manhood --
----

    absent of mind, shallow of thought.

Piss poor vision too.   Can't/won't see no
farther than

the next, maybe the last, sexual encounter

    or: mind-numbing high.

Contrary to popular beliefs – taller shoes
won't

make you a bigger man but they will mess up
ur foundation

and your mind in most cases.

Stumbling

   through what you believe is life,

with countless contradictions,

         contraptions,

         misconceptions,

   and   counteractions

as you are --- thinking (often stinking)
your/ourselves

Into unforgivable situations.

It's like fartin' in a tub of water –

and then biting the bubbles!

Just something to do –-- to pass the time

         while time passes you.

Introspection: Dig yourself. Answer the
phone, brother,

sister;

The answers are within you.

Give yourself a chance to give yourself a chance.

Realize that the mind of the world and

the world of the mind

have one thing in common – they can be changed.

And for the better if you'll negate your negative

destructive thoughts and actions.

Positive. Sometimes it's just a word.

Right now it's what we must be.

It ain't about no handshake,

or: how down your conversation be.

It's in your eye.

All it takes is a look.

And I didn't say peep and see.

Trying to peep through a keyhole

Wind up looking up an asshole

and can't see the fecal matter!

Look. And see. Look and see.

See who/what you are and realize that

that's who/ what you be.

Did I hear you say definance??

Defy your mind. Take a mental laxative.

Cleanse your mind of all distractions.

Purge your thoughts. That's where it begins.

Enter the realm of realization, of positive life
force.

Realize that life is a mind altering drug.

Be what your internal world says you are.

Not what the external world wants you to be.

Real is what I'm speaking of.

Real is what we've got to be.

That's

   defiance

     for your ass!

AIN'T THOSE HANDS COLD?

chains:

rope"

the first 2 nightmares we were

forced to deal with here.

here and then.

here and now.

here in this insane asylum called amerikkka.

chains:

      two cars in ur garage. (one for each
foot)

      a suit for everyday of the year.

      maybe we should put gran'ma in a
home.

      tennis anyone?

rope:

      Oh, God! There's a 'negro' in my
mirror!

(naw baby, somebody poured Bosco in
ur face powder)

African! Who, me??

man, I got 50-11 hoes out dere…(his
sisters)

a scholarship to Yale & all the poop u
can eat.

(dat negro got a big appetite, edsel)

break the bonds of ignorance!

they took'em off ur body

now it's time to

take'em off ur mind.

truth – like a giant jack hammer – beatin'

on the four corners of ur head.

U refuse to see the light.

U keep complainin' about Excedrin headache

number first.

and u trip on.

this ain't ur game.

these ain't ur rules.

but u can't understand

why u can't get a good hand.

(it's called strip poker)

shufflin' along singing ur song:

"trippin' thru a winter wonderland."

wonder what's wrong with ur ass.

winter is 4 seasons long in this country.

the abominable snowman has one golden
rule:

U gotta suck some to git some!

open ur eyes

befo' u git sucked out of this lie ur livin'

nicknamed existence.

What u call life is merely a product

of their perverted minds.

the snowman pulls ur string and u dance:

put ur foot in ur sister's ass.

(ain't those hands cold?)

the snowman pulls ur string and u sing:

boss, dey talkin' bout changing
things.

(ain't those hands cold?)

nothing is forever.

they find a brother who sings and dances
better than u.

the snowman cuts ur string off.

(weren't those hands cold?)

U become another Geraldine;

lookin' for somebody/thing to defend/offend
ur precious? ass.

and u trip on.

they got bigger chains:

intercontinental ballistic missiles and
batman.

they got longer rope:

FBI/CIA & the Mafia (it's all in the
family)

U still trippin on a brighter future –

a better tomorrow in amerikkka (chains)

and all the snowman is givin up

is instant oblivion if

ur not a good boy. (rope)

gittin u offa this dope (the great amerikkkan
dream)

is like

takin meat-flavored pop sickles

from dog-minded negros.

(can't git enough of that funky stuff)

        spit it out ur mouth.

        spit it out ur mind.

what can I do? (u cry)

U can defend urself if a man u truly be.

U can defend urself against these
homosexual ice machines.

U can scream rape – the way u gittin
screwed:

                over

                under

            around & thru

leave the chains

where u found them.

leave the rope

around the snowman's

neck.

U took'em off ur body –

take'em off ur mind

take'em off!!

take'em off for ur sake,

for ur mother's sake,

for ur sister's sake,

for ur children's sake,

do it for u/them

U know who to do it for,

but do u know who to do it to?

(I truly hope that u do)

Ain't those hands cold, brother?

ARE WE OR AREN'T WE?

(ONLY YOUR HEADSHRINKER KNOWS FOR SURE)

where is together?

why doesn't it occupy

our space---our time?

I thought that being

who and what we are

that this is how we would be…

together-----------------------but

I may be mistaken.

Imagine…

    A for real look,

        a for real smile,

            a casual

whisper (it's cool)

and your heart's at ease---

A fragment of nature totally at peace;

because you know that all's well.

everybody and everything is together.

one brother pulling another

out of a rut---

that might cost his but.

one sister pushing another

over a hump---

done selling her rump.

pushing-pulling in the same direction....

towards a common goal-

not gold.

A bond that's skin tight and deeper than

all past generations.

did I say tight?   damn right.

tighter than a preacher's poop chute! that's
righteously together.

where is together?

is it in plum nearly??

plum out of this world—

nearly out of this universe?

I think not.

not being who and what we are.

we are rhythm...

the pulse of all creation.

stepping, as one, towards our destiny.

gathering strength and momentum

with each rhythmic stride.

kicking holes in old realities..

leaving new ones in their places.

surging forward, ever forward, like a

mighty black ocean, reclaiming that which is
ours.

moving upward like mercury in a
thermometer

on a too hot day---------reaching for the sun.

one step at a time.

one mighty foot placed in front of the other.

Results: positive vibrations------------
Birthquakes!

everything not of us will fall/tumble,
dissolve/crumble

return to where ever it came from.

that be together!

Where is together?

It's in your heart if it beats;

It's in your mind if you think;

It's in our being, if we be.

blackbirds of a feather flying together

to the sun for the winter.

ridding ourselves of the past

even a cat buries its poop in the sand,

and proceeds to----------another level.

It ain't about yesterday, that's dead and
gone.

nothing's left but the present & the future;

one and the same:

just add E-R.

if today is bright, tomorrow will be brigh<u>ter</u>;

if we're strong today, tomorrow we'll be st>strong<u>er</u>.

can we get together?   that's the question.

is an elephant heavy?   that's the answer.

but we can't afford to forget:

If one doesn't come, the rest can't go—

If we don't get it together, there'll be

No

Show.

THE PURPOSE OF MIND

(a power boost)

Inhale: behavior-----

is the function of perception;

is the application of understanding:

your actions are dictated

by your analysis of your surroundings.

Exhale:

OMMMMMMMMMMMMMMMMMMMMMMM
MMMMMMM.......

inhale: infants and old folks have

one thing in common, total paranoia.

the infants

hang on to each of life's moments

remembering the joys and

not forgetting the pains

of the million-fold sights,

sounds, & sensations

that are their life's testimonies.

the aged

cling to memories and fleeting seconds

in fear and bewilderment.

Life has lost its fascination

and death does not arouse their curiosity.

Lost is the awareness that states:

     Living is to experience only half of life.

Exhale:

OMMMMMMMMMMMMMMMMMMMMMMM
MMMMMMM..........

in hell: to decipher human intellect

is of no great consequence.

to understand-----

the song of the birds,

the sound of the wind,

the dance of the waves,

the glare of the sun,

the precision of the heavens,

the laws of the universe,

the purpose of mind,

Is to

ex hell:

OMMMMMMMMMMMMMMMMMMMMMMMM
MMMMMM…….

'Our Father, who art in Heaven, amen"

THE SHADOWS OF MAN

You see them everyday of your life.

The lonely souls of our people

passing each other in the streets;

like dead leaves caught up in

the strong winds of misery and
despair.

You see them everyday of your life.

My brothers in their nods of
submission;

caught up in the vicious circle of

escaping the unescapable.

seeking to hide behind a flimsy curtain

of security while releasing the strength

of the mind, body and soul

through little holes in their arms.

You see them everyday of your life.

My brothers cruising the
neighborhoods

in their glamor-mobiles,

looking like a movie you saw last
week---

seeking admiration for being caught up
in

a physical/mental catastrophe.

You see them everyday of your life,

My sisters—the blessings of eternity,

looking at you with eyes that can no
longer shed tears

chained to the walls of lust and
passion for pay.

A being of love that no longer finds
love in being.

Cleopatra reduced to sexual servitude.

You see them everyday of your life.

My grandparents, and yours, fearfully

venturing from their homes to cash
their

social security checks—wondering what

forms of greed and cruel misfortune

await them on their perilous journey home.

You see them everyday of your life.

My older sisters boarding buses at 5 A.M.

going to the heights to clean mr. & mrs. White folks

home, top to bottom, for 15 dollars a day.

They return home, ankles swollen, backs aching,

sick and tired…………………..

she'll catch the bus at 5 A.M. tomorrow morning.

You see them everyday of your life.

My brothers and sisters leaving home
to

put in their eight hours of prostitution
for the man;

only to return home and discover that
some

loving soul has taken everything that
they owned;

except the rats and roaches.

You see them everyday of your life.

My brothers walking around with three
pistols,

and only two hands and one thought---

I can't trip with a dead head.

How long will it be before

my brothers realize that we share so much
more

than complexion and misfortune?

How long will it be before

my brothers begin to understand the
absolute,

 the relative, and the relationship between
the two?

How long will it be before

my brothers turn to the Son for guidance

and quit tripping over the Shadows of man?

MAKING
LOVE
TO
YOU

for JEANNETTA

speak my name…

and I hear the tender sound of snowflakes

falling.

the tender sigh of moonbeams

penetrating my world of dreams.

speak my name…

and I feel the ageless glory

of the Son rising

within my soul.

the everywhere-ness that is

the power of day & night.

speak my name…

speak my name…

and I become a lavender vision

in a land of Sugar Trees,

a timeless being kneeling

in the shadow of your Love.

speak my name...

and I see the silver reflections

of my childhood

laughter,

stars fall from the heavens,

their radiance overwhelmed by your own

speak my name...

and I know the bliss

of a perpetual moment.

Woman

Woman

was not created from man's head to be above him;

nor was she created from his heel to be trampled by him.

She was taken from his side to be near to him;

from beneath his arm to be protected by him;

from close to his heart to be loved by him.

Jeannetta, I truly love you.

Our Vows

Beautiful People, we are gathered here today, in full view of God, to ceremoniously join Jeannetta and Harry in the tender embrace of Matrimony, as they shall now exchange vows.

I vow to love, respect, care for and protect you as long as there is breath in my body, and as long as there is a beat in my heart;

I vow to hold your precious love, happiness and well being above all other factions in my life;

I vow to be your eternal husband (wife) in this life and those yet to come;

I vow to never forsake you in moments of great troubles or grave despair.

I vow to never allow the confusions of this world to contaminate the pure, spontaneous beauty that I see in this sacred experience called you;

These vows I make and promise to keep even after my spirit has once again become a part of the Absolute;

Let this ring symbolize the three hundred and sixty degree completeness of this love that I have for you;

May we be ever mindful of the Truth that One and One is One;

By the power vested in me by the Absolute, the Relative and the relationship between the two, I now pronounce you ONE.....

My Bride

I am blessed most every morning
    for if by chance I crack an eye
I may behold a sight of wonder
    I speak true – I dare not lie.

You are the sister of my soul
    my eternal lover – my loving bride
But when I watch you as you're sleeping
    I see mother nature at my side.

The sun ascends from your left breast
    after sleeping through the night
At even time I gaze in wonder
    as it nestles in your right.

I watch you rise without much effort
    as you subdue the mirror's stare

With fluid strokes and easy motion

you comb the stars out of your hair.

In your eyes I see a promise

of countless dreams I must fulfill

I humbly submit these to my Master

They shall be done – be it His will.

I beg of you both faith and patience

in me and what I hold as true

With your sweet love and His guidance

I shall realize these dreams for you.

With my strength, my clever nature

and my devotion to the three

I shall conquer all my shortcomings

and love you with a love that's free.

Love free of fear and intimidation

Love free of pain and misery

Love free of pitfalls from my ego

Love free of all that is not free

Love free of prejudice and suffering

Love free of jealousy and greed

Love free of lust and temptation

Love tailored to your every need.

If by chance you have not figured

out these heart/felt words of mine

I am simply trying to tell you

I love you, 'til the end of time.

OUR THANKS TO YOU

As Mother Earth Cherishes

the Sun's Rays

We shall Cherish your

gift for Always

MAKING LOVE TO YOU

Is like…

Hey! Let me put it this way:

In the beginning, which began with

    You and I,

We created the heavens and the earth;

And everything therein.

And after we had made everything in the known

And unknown world, we realized that there was only

One thing that we had not made. Love!

We had not made Love!!

And in the presence of the only true beings in the

Universe, all of creation blushed and smiled and said

Unto us, "yes, in the name of all that is good, sweet

Pure and correct, we beg of you----make love."

We knew what we must do.

And with the speed of thought

                    I made my plea

unto you.

Your answer to me?
    "sure"

Therein the word PLEASURE was born,
along with its

                Many sensations.

We had no time to waste, how could we
waste time?

Time was/is our creation.

We began to perform the dance of love.

We assumed the position of the world
passionately.

When I entered you the birds began to sing;

so did you.

Then there was no more of me to give

And you could take no more:

We were full of each other.

Slowly we began to move.

Thus the world was set into motion;

Sweet blissful, perpetual motion.

The stars took their places in the heavens.

This is merely a poetic expression

But we were/are poetry.

And we mad love:

> over mountains, through valleys.

> Across the burning sands—in the
freezing snow.

> From continent to continent.

> From constellation to constellation.

We made love throughout the
known/unknown world.

The universe almost crumbled beneath the
strain.

As we neared the end of our endless journey

The earth began to shake;

lions roared; birds sought the shelter of
the trees.

The universe tried to hide within itself!

As our bodies and souls eternal were
bombarded by eons of sensation.

And when you came volcanoes erupted;

Mountains fell into the sea!

Oceans, rivers, streams and brooks began to
flow

Over/around/through hills and valleys

Down your thighs.

When we had finished I took your smile and

Placed it in the heavens

It became the rainbow;

an arch proclaiming love eternal

And the sky wept tears of joy/fulfillment.

The fine dew covered the pits of black heat

That were our bodies.

But it could never extinguish our everlasting fire.

I leaned near to you and whispered

       'precious, the world needs nothing more"

You smiled once again

And so it was,

Making love to the world.

DELIRIOUS JOY

you reduce my contact impressions:

temperature, pressure, pain.

your touch supplies the rewards

that my sensibilities require:

higher intellectual and emotional stimulation.

your fragrance intrigues me.

captivating. liberating.

i smell the aromas of unity

and divine purpose.

i smell freedom within you.

you kiss me tenderly

and my appetites are satisfied.

i savor your flavor,

dutch chocolate honey.

bees are confused.

my gaze encounters you

and sight suddenly has a reason.

you provide my vision;

extraordinary beauty;

succulent eye candy.

you say my name.

i marvel as
the syllables

cling delicately to your lips,

sensing my ear's addiction

to your luscious lyrical wine.

you engulf my senses in delirious joy.

REFLECTIONS

IRENE

Allow me to create, if I may

A picture of peace, so serene;

Negating both paints and canvas

I now render a portrait of Irene.

As a member of human kind

Her life has been filled with strife;

Yet within the walls of her battered soul

Burn the fires of compassion, love and life.

Her travels led her down a perilous road;

Many sisters have stumbled upon it.

She didn't't become bitter or phony,

She can say, "I love you" and mean it.

Her majestic virtue is "understanding."

She possesses the fire of the stars.

She has dealt with many hardships,

Her tattered Spirit still bears the scars.

She lends her shoulder to absorb your tears,

As she plugs into your mind.

She exploits both her ability to listen

And her capacity to be kind.

She is the fountain of Nature's Joy,

Her waters are sweet and refined.

She stands atop a mountain of love,

A monument to woman-kind.

My deeper thoughts of the Queen – Mother

Cannot in words be expressed.

When I think of all that she has been to me,

The total of my being is impressed.

A toast to you:

May the Sun – your Father in the sky smile upon your humble Spirit;

And may nothing but oceans of love dampen the shores of your Soul…

This kiss is for you

PERSEVERE

(for my Jeannetta and the Angelic Four)

We are the flames of Sisterhood,

we are the Angelic Four;

inspired by A.K.A.'s togetherness

we knock humbly at your door.

        (four ivies

stand before you,

        four angelic

hearts sincere;

        this truth we

have discovered,

        we have but

to persevere.

Stripped of all concepts of self

this pearl of wisdom we've kept;

a journey of one thousand miles

begins with the first step.

(four ivies

stand before you,

four angelic

hearts sincere;

this truth we

have discovered,

we have but

to persevere.)

A.K.A. is a mystical place,

a land beyond the Sun;

we are ever marching towards you

'til our victory is won...

(four ivies

stand before you,

four angelic

hearts sincere,

this truth we

have discovered,

we have but

to persevere.)

We are ivies of humility

ignoring our ego's calls;

our only selfish ambition is

to tread those sacred halls…

            (four ivies

stand before you,

            four angelic

hearts sincere;

            this truth we

have discovered,

            we have but

to persevere.)

UNTITLED

infinite; blackness; total; complete.

traces of stardust

gleam in your eyes.

humane/ness

burns deep

within your heart.

secrets of life

illuminate your being.

                    I stand before the alter...

microcosmic universe.

conveyor of life.

black star shining brightest.

midnight drums.

throbbing rhythm.

echoes from the womb.

your heart beats

the intricate patterns

of my simple

love song

           I bend my knees in

worship…

mother/sister/daughter mine.

you are

seasons 4

directions 4

winds 4

love 4 me

4ces of nature

fire: devastating

water: penetrating

wind: separating

earth: emancipating

you are power supreme

           I bow my head in prayer.

WINGS OF LIGHT

(for Nanny)

Sweet Prince of the Morning

a new Angel has entered your realm of Eternal Life

to her be gentle, she has borne her share of Strife

Heavenly Father, give this Angel Wings of Light.

Sweet Prince of the Morning

may you keep this Angel close to your loving breast

she has done your Will on earth; she needs her rest

Heavenly Father, give this Angel Wings of Light.

Sweet Prince of the Morning

she has known her share of heartaches and
fears

I know that you will tenderly kiss away her
tears

Heavenly Father, give this Angel Wings of
Light.

Sweet Prince of the Morning

we shall miss her more than any words can
tell

we won't worry 'cause we know You'll keep
her well

Heavenly Father, give this Angel Wings of
Light.

ONE + ONE + ONE = THREE

the essence of knowledge is confusion.

it heralds your entrance into this world;

it hounds you throughout your term of life;

it hides your exit when your moment here is
spent;

Confusion is in you.

you are the essence...

the awakening of knowledge is curiosity.

it motivates your finite thoughts and actions;

it incubates your unique creative abilities;

it compels you to seek your purpose for
being;

Curiosity is in you.

you are the awakening...

the light of knowledge is Truth.

it represents the dictator that governs your life;

it provides the constant in life that is never-ending;

it is the child of the cosmos – the eternal life that you seek;

Truth is in you.

you are the light…

and light is not afraid to shine.

MIRROR

the incorrect application of knowledge

as opposed to

the correct application of ignorance.

which is the true

Image/reflection?

FINALE

TAKE YOUR PRAISE

what's it going to be

my brothers and sisters?

You've journeyed countless miles

to become misses and misters.

You've struggled hard to integrate

the mainstream of white life;

enduring incessant degradation,

turmoil and strife.

Take your praise.

Our consciousness we must raise

so that the world might see.

To remind others, as well as ourselves,

the true definition of free.

Within our pain racked souls

the light of truth awaits,

one of our mighty chieftain

to open the ebony gates,

to let that light escape,

as we conceive a brighter fate.

Take your praise.

Imprisoned by our mental anguish

we desperately cling to hope

but as long as we remain in lock-up

we're like germs under a scope.

When in reality we can transform

our unfortunate conditions,

and proceed to establish ourselves

in our predestined positions.

To let the world know who,

what, why we are.

Our family continues nothing less than

bright and shining Stars

Take your praise.

The roads we've traveled

have been rough and

the directions have been many.

We struggle for basic humane rights,

and we are told we can't get any.

With our blood, sweat, and tears

we've made amerikkka the king.

Now it's time to reveal this country

as a very unnatural thing.

Without our slave labor

Amerikkka wouldn't be.

Come on brothers and sisters

Won't you dare to be free?

Take your praise.

Sever the bonds that tie your mind

to this exploitative game.

Considering who, what, why we are

it's a crying shame;

to see brothers and sisters

whose minds still pick cotton,

cringing behind doors, in dark corners

all dreams of our future forgotten,

Times are harder now than they've been,

That truth I must admit.

If we channel our hands and our hearts

we can straighten out some shit.

Take your praise.

When you become ex-niggers

and listen to your mind,

you'll discover our purpose here

is to better human kind.

Originally earth was a paradise

designed to support us ALL;

We have yielded to mass deception

contributing to our own fall.

We have so much more in common

than twist of fate and misery,

but once we get it together

we will again dominate history!

Take your praise.

Awaken mighty sleeping giant

and let the task begin.

Let us put our house in order

and bring dissension to an end.

Get down the way that we know we can;

create that "family" feeling.

Brothers and sisters we've got to

stop "dealin" and start "dealing."

Grab the bull by the tail and

calmly face this situation,

bearing in mind that on the t.v.

of life you can't change the station.

We need to pool our vast resources,

throughout this entire nation.

and ignoring all external distractions,

create our own t.v. station!!

Take your praise.

The song that I sing herein

Attempts to single out the lie

That has been generated to/thru us

When the truth will get us by.

Black people, you're so rare, so fine

And I'm glad that you're mine;

So rare, so fine, I'm glad that youre mine;

So rare, so fine, I'm so glad...

Take your praise.

Eulogy for Quentin Rasputin Reynolds
Cockroach III

Dearly beloved---

We are gathered here today,

to send this bad little insect

on his merry way.

Quentin Rasputin Reynolds Cockroach III

was this roach's name,

doing what he damn well pleased

was his claim to fame.

It was a rainy day in august

the sun had barely shone;

the way the story was related to me

Quentin was born full-grown!

Did you hear what I told you?

This roach was never a child;

my brother found him in his kitchen

smoking' reefer, runnin' wild.

Astonished by the sight he saw

this is what he told me.

'you know, that had to be the prettiest roach

my eyes did ever see.

He wore a pair of blue suede shoes,

a fu Manchu adorned his lip,

he had diamonds on his feelers,

a straight razor on his hip.

He sported a red velvet waistcoat

with emeralds down the side;

The sweet smell of English leather

scented his ebony hide.

A player he must have at one time been

for he had women by the pair.

And you should have seen how carefully

they took the rollers from his hair.

Bear with me though I know you're restless,

this eulogy has just begun.

I've got to tell you about this roach

and of the deeds he's done.

My brother came home late one night

he wasn't feelin' bad.

He heard a growl and saw to his surprise

his dog had gone stone mad!

This huge Doberman was standin' there

foamin' at the lips;

My brother fought with all his might

to keep his bowels within his hips.

The red-eyed dog leaped across the room

and pinned him to the floor.

Then there came a sharp, splintering sound

as someone kicked down the door.

Need I say that without this intrusion

the situation would've been gory...

But silhouetted in the torn up doorway

stood Quentin in his glory.

He said, "I don't know what the problem is

but I'm tryin' to get some sleep,

Now when I walk out of this room

I don't expect to hear a peep."

And as these solemn words of his

echoed through the gloom

That kill-crazed Doberman pincher

went charging across the room.

Quentin saw him coming and side stepped

to let him past.

As the dog shot by, Quentin screamed and

kicked him 7 times in the ass!

This caught the dog completely unaware, he
turned

and snapped at the roach.

And with blinding speed Quentin drew his
razor

and cut the animal's throat!

With the deed done he said to my brother,

"I've no-doubt saved your life.

Now if you don't want to deal with me

you'll have to pay my price.

I want the largest room in the house

I don't want no static,

As far as the furniture is concerned you can

stick it in the attic.

Play me some music night and day,

I dig the Philly sound.

I want a box of sugar every morning.

I want my reefer by the pound."

My brother couldn't believe what he heard as he

lay sweating on the floor.

Quentin casually turned around and pimped

slowly through the door.

The weeks passed, the demands were met

and Quentin became a star.

But true to his insatiable desires

that roach went too far!

Brother came home one afternoon

and found his daughter quite upset,

It appears that Quentin was feeling' his fluid

and had mannishly torn her dress.

Now bro couldn't believe his ears,

he was somewhat beside himself.

He dashed blindly to his bedroom closet and

took his .45 from the shelf.

He ran angrily to his daughter's room

and found Quentin on her bed;

And before Quentin could pull his razor, Bro

bounced 7 bullets off his head!

Let us pray

Father we thank you for your gifts of love,

these words our hearts must say;

But we thank this lowly cockroach

for bringing us here today---

Amen

CONTINUATION

OF

A

MAN

COME WALK WITH ME

So many years of my youth filled with blood, fights and pain......

Felt good to be delivered from the shackles and chains.....

Now come walk with me............

I first got jumped when I was 5 years old......

So no wonder I lived with a heart that was cold...... Like the snow I walked through after school.....

Before I was kicked and stumped by 4th, 5th, and 6th graders......

But all I hear is silence when I asked my Creator....... Why?

Come walk with me

That's why I don't trust people now.....

Now get from behind me before you get knocked out....

When I was 8 years old that little girl lied,

Then her 16 year old brother, that was 5 times my size.....

Whooped on me because of untruthful words spoken,

I thank God I walked away without any bones broken.......

Come walk with me........

Living in poverty.......

Pop tarts and eggs.... Mostly what was eaten.....

And to be an eye witness to a man brutally beaten...... with a baseball bat.... Up against the passenger side front tire......

His arms were flopping like stereo speaker wires..... But he didn't make a sound.......

His face was not recognizable as he was beaten down......... It's like time sloowwwweeeed dooooowwwwwnnnn...........

I didn't understand what I was seeing.....

I couldn't believe the man was still breathing.....

But thank God He gave him strength to get up....... I'll say it again, thank God He gave him the strength to get up!!!!!!!

He stood up and ran and his arm was still flopping...

He ran like Jesse Owens and it was no stopping......

So then Pops backed the car up......

I was in shock and just witnessed the impossible

Then Pops said "Bro get in, I'll take you to the hospital"......

Come walk with me.....

PRISON TO POWER

Last call for alcohol...... the soft legs that I see......

I'm feeling good after all...... this Long island iced tea.....

With this black and mild cigar to smoke until the last hour....

Hoping my mind can escape from prison to power.......

While I'm still at the club.......

I'm dying from having this institutionalized mind......

Locked up mentally and spiritually blind....

Well let me just pray before I have sex with this lady....

I pray I don't catch nothing or that she has my baby......

Back to the emergency room I go.......

I'm tired of the pain and tired of the struggle....

I'm tired of drunk nights that led to one night stand trouble....

Hungover with lust.... filled with hate and disgust....

She's talking about marriage and we don't have trust......

She don't even know my real name...... And what's your name again?

Trapped in this worldly way of thinking.....

Trying to get rid of my problems with smoking and drinking......

I'm tired of beer with double shots of liquor by the hour....

Time to get out of this prison and move into power...

I accepted Jesus Christ as my Lord and savior.....

Now I have peace of mind without any drinks......

The superb mental clarity that I have when I think.....

The spiritual strength I gained and being empowered to preach.........

The knowledge from God being used to teach...

What a breath of fresh air......

Everlasting life, praising God through song....

Being able to forgive others when there actions are wrong.....

No more smoking or drinking but living my life for God,

Righteousness is why I'm here and my name is Rashaad.....

Righteous Sin Cleanser is the meaning of my name.....

Last call…. Last call!!! But this time not for alcohol….

No more one night stands, time to praise God afterall!

Time to keep preaching and show people The Way,

I'll always speak truth no matter what others may say…..

Thank God for my transition from prison to power.

FROM GRACE TO ETERNITY

(Grandma)

When you're walking that road of righteousness that seems too much to bare,

And you decide to confess with your mouth and believe in your heart in prayer.

God is smiling......

And grace, favor and power are His essence,

To be absent from the body means that you are in His presence.

But I wish you were still here......

Sweet like sugar, just the way God made ya,

With such a sweet spirit that reminds me of our savior.

I still remember when you use to make your banana pudding......

Asking me to come pray for you when you had trouble breathing,

Praying through the pain and you never stopped believing.

The good Lord was always with you.....

You were blessed and highly favored and full of amazing grace,

You allowed Christ to be the author and finisher of your faith......

The strength of one of God's mighty children.....

That's how I know you got your wings...... And you're in a heavenly place,

And are present with the almighty and can see God face to face.........

And you have been taken from grace....... to eternity.

MY WIFE OF FAITH

You are the woman I prayed for,

I'm the man you were made for,

I promise to love you better than I did
yesterday.....

I promise to comfort and protect you til death
do us part. ..

As long as God gives me breath to
breathe.......you will always have my heart

Because you are the love of my life....

God is the head of Christ, Christ the head of
man and man the head of woman......
and......

God is love...

Christ is the Word......

So I promise to stay in the Word so that Love is the head and ruler over the Word that's in me......

That way I can always love you the way that God wants me too.....

Faith brought us together,

Faith will keep us together,

Faith lead us in love,

And we will stay in love if we keep falling in love....... with Jesus

MY WALKING MIRACLE

(For the love of my life, my lovely wife
Racheal)

Where are you!!!! Are you ok? Can you feel
your legs?!!!!! As I try to keep it together!!

Then she says "Babe, I don't know......
they're taking me on a stretcher".......

(Silence).........

As my heart skips beats, voice cracking as I
speak.....

I held my cell phone that was fully powered
but I felt powerless and weak......

In that hourless moment...... God can you fix
this? Is what I was wondering.

As I held back my frustration with God to
keep my voice from thundering.....

I prayed.......

I know Your Word says we're accounted for
all day for the slaughter,

But Lord please heal my wife, we have a 4 month old daughter....

As I hurried to the hospital......

My wife was in the trauma unit and my heart starts beating faster,

I couldn't help but to brace myself for the worst disaster

The nurse comes to get me and takes me to the back then to the left.....

And before I see my wife...... I take one more last breath.......

Our eyes connect, she's smiling, my heart is no longer filled with grief,

My miracle is going to live and walk, what a sigh of relief....

The doctor comes to check on her and asks if she's ok?

He says he's never seen an accident like this and doesn't know what to say.....

He said a tire went through your windshield and you have a concussion.

If you don't remember much, that's ok no need for discussion.

You can go home and rest..........

We were given the discharge papers and soon after we left.

We went to gather her things from the car....... All of her belongings were still there....

And when I seen the vehicle, I couldn't help but cry and stare... As I just stood there.......

Speechless.....

Uncontrollably emotional with an inexplicable meekness.....

Thanking God for His protection!!! He's invisible but not far!!

Then I asked my wife, how in the world did you get out the car?

She said I don't know, but I'm still here baby please don't cry.

She takes her non-injured hand to wipe my teary eye.

I thank God you're still here!
I thank God you're still walking!
I thank God you're still breathing!
I thank God you're still talking!
My walking miracle!!!!

MY HUMBLE CRY

I come before you Lord,
Praying that you hear my cry,
I do many wrongful things and Lord
I really do not know why.

It's so easy to do what I hate,
But so hard to do what's right,
I hope you forgive me before it's too late,
I must remember that it's not my fight.

I pray you give me strength,
And that I'm not easily deceived,
So I can touch the souls and hearts of those,
That really do not believe.

It's probably people who cry out loud,
Whose prayers you do not hear,
We must remember not to pray in crowds,
And that it's YOU that we must fear.

Throughout my life, I myself
Have done many sinful things,
But I'm thankful for the joy
And all the blessings that YOU bring.

I pray for knowledge and understanding,
For things you may arrange,
I pray for serenity
To accept things I cannot change.

The courage to change the things I can
And the wisdom so that I know,
When I'm supposed to take it fast
And when I'm supposed to take it slow.

I pray for those that do not know,
That it is all a test of faith,
We must be saved and baptized with Christ,
In order to win this race.

Many of us are conformed to this world,
All across the globe,
Can we have the faith, courage,
And strength you gave to Job?

See the Lord Jesus Christ,
Gave His life to save us all,
So when it feels like your down and out
With your back against the wall....

Stay patient in tribulation

And constant in prayer,
And realize that when you cry….
The Lord is always there.

Through crucifixion we must die,
Through resurrection we shall live,
And the gift of eternal life
Is for you, the Lord shall give.

The only thing guaranteed in Life,
Is that one day the flesh will die.
So I ask you Lord for forgiveness,
And that you hear "My Humble Cry."

KEEP ME AWAY FROM THE WOLVES

Keep me away from the wolves, for I am a sheep,

They're counting on my sheep wools, give me strength when I'm weak

Build me up when I'm torn down when there's tears that I shed

Forgive me for my sins when I live misled.

Although I'm not?

The Word of God tells me what to do and what not....

So keep me away from the wolves, and the cold weather

I pray I don't stray from you Lord as my shepherd

When the wolves attack, I fight back with this sword

And the Lord of my life protects me from the scorn,

Yes, those imitations of life....

The devil wants to confuse and misuse you for things that are trife

Not for those things that are Christ like

So you need God's protection to keep yo'life right.

To stay away from those wolves, I don't want to die in sin

So when the Lord returns again, I want to have earned my way in and be forgiven for my sins

So that my soul.......

Will be blessed with eternal...... Happiness

Notes pg 61 - Mirrors

x 68/9
pg 64 - Take Your Praise

pg 77 Come walk w/me

pg 88 My Walking Miracle

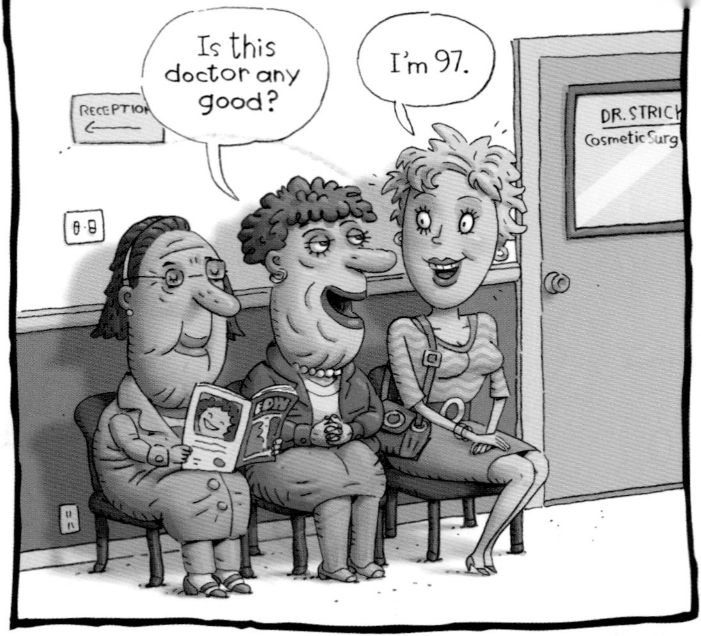

THURSDAY | APRIL 13, 2017

It's a pretty picture but the first thing is the scripture....

Your Sword and your armor will be tested and pulled

But this is what's needed to protect you from the wolves.

LORD TELL ME WHY

Lord tell me why I shed tears when there's no pain

Lord tell me why I want to be sheltered when there is no rain

Why do I fear death when you protect me all the day long

Why is it hard to do right when I know what I do is wrong

My days will be long upon the land My Lord my God giveth me,

Because I honor my mother and father, this is what you have promised me

Why is it that I've come a long way but yet, have so much more to do

Fear not what I know I shall suffer, but I don't want to die before my parents do

Lord tell me why we're born crying while everybody's smiling.....

Lord tell me why everyone's crying when we die smiling.....

Is it because of the trials, tribulations and treacherous times to come?

Is it because of temptations and the devil trying to take us from.....

You Lord...... So please tell me why

My cousin is facing 17 years, it makes me want to cry

I know we all have sinned and there's only one that was sinless,

That's why I'm thankful for your blessings as I ask for your forgiveness

I'll always praise your name, I'll praise you til the day I die,

But I have so many questions, so Lord please tell me why.

LORD W.A.R.S.

I want you to know what the words "LORD W.A.R.S. means,

Lord Will Always Reign Supreme, see

You got nice clothes, food and freedom but your still whining,

While smiling in the Summer when the Sun's shining,

But it's snowing......

The chimes are silent but yet the wind's blowing..

Did you get dat?

The Lord has blessed you much, but you still complain,

Thinking He hasn't protected you from the rain,

But you're not wet......

Turbulent times come, life doesn't seem too nice

Have you forgotten all things can be done through Christ?

Who's the Lord of your life?

Is it sex, drinking, memories of getting high?

Brothas focusing on the prize between the thighs.....

Of that beautiful young lady........

Having sex with you but is about to have your homeboy's baby... Did you get dat?

Weed, envy, pride, and lust!!!

Trying to become the lover of someone you can't trust,

What kinda sense does that make?

Who's the Lord of your life?

Greed, money, bragging about how you got laid,

But in reality it's the Lord and yourself you've betrayed.....

Caring about sex and how much you got paid,

Is it then the devil the Lord that you praise?

Who's the Lord of your life?

Anger, hatred, revenge, animosity,

A life that is filled with curiosity.....

You know that killed the cat.....

Speaking of cats, they're sneaky, deceiving, conniving,

Always wondering what kinda car is he driving?

How much money he make?

Can he cook and bake cake?

"I like shrimp and steak"....... Honey....

You got champagne taste with minimum wage beer money!!!

Who's the Lord of your life!!!

Without the almighty God, how can you survive,

It's like trying to breed a cat without 9 lives

See, the battle over self is where the LORD W.A.R.S. begin, and for the 1st lesson,

To sin or not to sin is the big question.

My Guiding Light

(For momma - Jeannetta)

Do what you can today because tomorrow's
not guaranteed…..

One of many life lessons you taught led to
two Masters' degrees….

You taught me how to pray and taught me
the Lord's prayer,

You told me He'd never leave me and that
He'd always be there….

You told me my gray hair was for wisdom
and I was just like Chuck,

My great grand daddy who taught me how to
play tonk….

You told me to confess when I'm wrong and
that I'd be a better man…..

Til this day I speak truth the best way that I can....

The seed you planted blossomed slowly, but then it grew faster...

Whoever though that bad boy from Pittsburgh would grow to be a Pastor.

You taught me to be faithful to whoever I marry in life...

Therefore I am faithful and never cheated on my wife....

If it weren't for your prayers, and the sacrifices you made...

To get me through college with the high tuition you paid.....

Where would I be? In your basement maybe?

Still married and in love with my little
newborn baby?.....

If it weren't for your prayers, and the things
that you've said

It if weren't for your prayers I'd most likely be
dead....

Thanks for teaching me life lessons... you
taught me the good fight

While I walk in Pops shadow.... Momma...
you are my guiding light.

Shadows of "A" Man

I reflect you in different ways,

As I pray for better days as I still learn how
the game plays,

The shadows of a man.....

I paid attention and followed you throughout
life,

I learned how to be a man and how a man
should love his wife,

The shadows of a man.....

You taught me to be a giver and to be of
good service,

So I present myself with love although I still
make people nervous,

The shadows of a man.....

You taught me how to throw my hands to
fight and to be a man of my word...

You taught me the loudest person is not right
and that silence can be heard.

The shadows of a man.....

You taught me a man knows who to mess
with and who not to question....

After I knocked a few out, I really learned that
lesson......

The shadows of a man....

You told me not to slump when I walk.....
make sure there's a purpose when I speak...

Strong eye contact at all times, a sign of
confidence in me......

The shadows of a man

You told me it was booty here before I was
born when I began my freshman year,

That fine sista in the elevator was smiling
from ear to ear.....

The shadows of a man....

You told me booty will be here when I die
and not to play the fool,

And if I focus on women like that fine sista
and flunk out of school? Then I'm on my
own.....

The shadows of a man....

I strive for your intellectual ability to be a
stone thrower,

A mind blower..... and as a preacher a seed
sower,

The shadows of a man.....

A unique philosopher of words as you
eloquently spoke,

You captured the minds and hearts of those
who listened as you'd smoke,

The shadows of a man....

The way you loved family and friends taught me how to love people,

Taught me to be respectful, to love and not be neglectful…...

The shadows of a man…..

What could be more powerful than the last words that we shared,

Simultaneously…. We spoke together and said the Lord's prayer…..

The shadows of a man….

60224727R00067

Made in the USA
Lexington, KY
30 January 2017